A Moment's Longing

A Moment's Longing

Haiku Society of America
Members' Anthology
2019

Tanya McDonald
Editor

A Moment's Longing

ISBN 978-0-930172-18-3

Each poem in this anthology was chosen by the editor from a selection of unpublished haiku and senryu submitted by current members of the Haiku Society of America. Each participating member has one poem in the anthology.

Cover photo: John L. Matthews
Cover design: Tanya McDonald
Layout: Tanya McDonald

Introduction

Welcome to the 2019 Haiku Society of America Members' Anthology. It has been an honor and an absolute delight to work on this collection of haiku and senryu.

The 441 poets represented in these pages hail from 47 states and 14 countries. For some, this is their very first publication. For others, it's not. While past anthologies have included previously-published poems, I decided to do things differently this year and only solicit unpublished poems. That way, everyone—novice and experienced poet alike—is in the same boat. Every poem in here (to the best of my knowledge) is making its worldwide debut on these pages.

Thank you to Michael Dylan Welch and Ignatius Fay for sharing their knowledge of InDesign, and to C. R. Manley for proofreading. My gratitude to the HSA executive committee for trusting me with this year's anthology. Thanks to John L. Matthews for the use of his photo on the cover. And thank you to Russell McDonald for his enduring support, and for listening to me ramble about this project since the daffodils were in bloom.

Enjoy the poems!

Tanya McDonald
August 27, 2019

following
a bend in the road
somewhere a meadowlark

Peggy Hale Bilbro
Huntsville, Alabama

a yellow kayak
on rippling blue—the paddler
carves infinity

Vicki McCullough
Vancouver, British Columbia

the summer
we were pirates
seafront cannon

frances angela
London, England

wild strawberries!
she'll always be
the youngest

Randy Brooks
Taylorville, Illinois

ghost story the smell of burnt marshmallow

Bob Lucky
Jubail, Eastern Province, Saudi Arabia

camping safari
waiting for the rain
to make love

Lew Watts
Chicago, Illinois

waking on the porch
the summer snow
of moonlight

Melissa Clarke Ward
Sisters, Oregon

Summer evening
eating a peach
the color of the moon

Sylvia Forges-Ryan
North Haven, Connecticut

a field of brambles
a promise
of blackberry pies

Dean Summers
Renton, Washington

morning commute
my breakfast of daydreams
leaping with trout

Michael McClintock
Clovis, California

fish hook in his brow
first aid kit
still on the list

Nancy Bright
Sisters, Oregon

lichen clinging
to rock / our
shallow lives

Sarah Paris
San Francisco, California

mirror lake
call and response
of two loons

Paulette Y. Johnston
Santa Fe, New Mexico

downshift
the mountain
in the mirror

Tom Painting
Atlanta, Georgia

early morning
the sound of the sprinkler
before the heat

Johnnie Johnson Hafernik
San Francisco, California

cicadas at dusk
the rocking chair's
rhythmic creak

Agnes Eva Savich
Austin, Texas

cafe ceiling fan
whirling
in her spoon

Gretchen Graft Batz
Elsah, Illinois

empty nest —
the flap flap of wings
in my chest

Marilyn Fleming
Pewaukee, Wisconsin

an inkblot of crows
settles in the hay field
month with no rain

Ferris Gilli
Marietta, Georgia

blue blood super same moon

Marsh Muirhead
Bemidji, Minnesota

Spring
the burnt out U
on the UHAUL sign

Mike Montreuil
Ottawa, Ontario

country road
a pothole
floats a feather

Susan Constable
Parksville, British Columbia

peony patch
no money
for dance lessons

Alexis Rotella
Arnold, Maryland

spring field
the pop underfoot
of missed cranberries

Eric Arthen
Worthington, Massachusetts

in the finger hole
of the shakuhachi
a spiderweb

Dyana Basist
Santa Cruz, California

cutting the bath valve
one final drop

Chris Graves
Halifax, Nova Scotia

telephone pole
the woodpecker still using
Morse code

Annette Makino
Arcata, California

the click
of worry beads
ice-sheathed branches

Susan B. Auld
Arlington Heights, Illinois

train passing at night
muffled by distance . . .
just crickets

Paul Sleman Clark
Kensington, Maryland

downsizing—
my old tap shoes
lost in the shuffle

Susan Godwin
Madison, Wisconsin

two women
in the lunch room
the ping of texting

Marcyn Del Clements
Claremont, California

near the shore
a seal chomps floating ice
broken silence

Janice Doppler
Easthampton, Massachusetts

Eclipse
one smoke ring
inside the other

Garry Gay
Santa Rosa, California

magma-twilight . . .
an orange hue half-lights
my neighbors' faces

brett brady
Haiku, Hawaii

glowing in the heart
of a charred Notre Dame . . .
the golden cross

Rebecca Drouilhet
Picayune, Mississippi

the stained glass
geometry
of autumn

S.M. Kozubek
Harbert, Michigan

gathering lime
watermelon lit clouds fall
in neon rain

∂mperez
San Antonio, Texas

sunset rays
cleave to Sandia Mountains
ripen with color

John J. Candelaria
Corrales, New Mexico

late spring —
still longing for my first
cherry blossom poem

Elizabeth Martens
Philadelphia, Pennsylvania

cool enough
to let my hair fly free
ocean breeze

Joette Giorgis
Port St. Lucie, Florida

wild irises!
the soft growl
of an unseen dog

Crystal Simone Smith
Durham, North Carolina

crossing the road
she holds her purple hijab
against the wind

Patricia Prime
Auckland, New Zealand

moon
in the
plums
warm
to the
touch

David Kāwika Eyre
Volcano, Hawaiʻi

rain-soaked woods
decorated with frogs
the boy's yellow boots

Adelaide B. Shaw
Somers, New York

pussy willows —
little children tickle
the cat's toes

Joanne M. Reinbold
Wilmington, Delaware

first rose —
my toddler's breath
parting the petals

Michael Dylan Welch
Sammamish, Washington

dinosaur exhibit
the voice of my grandson
so tiny

Charles Trumbull
Santa Fe, New Mexico

surviving artifacts
noses pressed against
plexiglass

Tom Sacramona
Plainville, Massachusetts

baby blanket
held together
with memories

Dean Okamura
Torrance, California

first petals
my nephew aces
his driving test

Erin Castaldi
Mays Landing, New Jersey

quinceañera
tears in papi's eyes
as we waltz

Renee Londner
Prospect, Connecticut

among
my mother's keepsakes
my first poem

Carolyn M. Hinderliter
Phoenix, Arizona

first person plural
still conjugating
my love for you

Michele Root-Bernstein
East Lansing, Michigan

wedding quilt
each butterfly square
a scrap of memory

Merle D. Hinchee
Houma, Louisiana

days after Christmas
one daughter's gifts still wrapped
beneath the tree

Lee Strong
Rochester, New York

the white knuckles
of the pollarded plane tree
first snow

Gregory Longenecker
Pasadena, California

plodding through drifts —
the Doppler shift
of each passing car

Paul Hendricks
Missoula, Montana

bent to the ground
the snow-laden cherry branches
I couldn't reach in summer

Seren Fargo
Bellingham, Washington

driving snow —
the wind's hollow voice
asks for respite

Patricia J. Machmiller
San Jose, California

under his breath
a few more names
for snow

Sarah E. Metzler
Marion Center, Pennsylvania

mountain snow
my hardest edges
revealed

Scott Wiggerman
Albuquerque, New Mexico

freezing fog
the ganglia
of trees

Ann K. Schwader
Westminster, Colorado

april icicle
    under
    the overpass

Scott Glander
Glenview, Illinois

winter rain
an old coat
of crows

Bill Gottlieb
Trinidad, California

cold that settles
deep in the neck
river bend

Glenn G. Coats
Carolina Shores, North Carolina

rough news
the windshield wipers
thud over ice

Marilyn Appl Walker
Madison, Georgia

deep snow
only the tips
of crosses

Robert B McNeill
Winchester, Virginia

my friend's funeral
my scarf from the country
he escaped from

Deanna Tiefenthal
Rochester, New York

Sunset colors darken —
Out of nowhere
A crescent moon

Mike Freiling
Portland, Oregon

grief counselling
a black cat
follows me home

Lucy Whitehead
Southend-on-Sea, Essex, England

death next door
all the family
she never saw

Roger Watson
Hull, East Yorkshire, England

Varanasi gloom
the acrid sting
of funeral pyre smoke

Jay Friedenberg
New York, New York

falling leaves
the light
between

Valorie Broadhurst Woerdehoff
Dubuque, Iowa

Haiku Poetry Day
ocean fog onto the island
fills with light

Bruce Ross
Hampden, Maine

A hole in the clouds —
mossy oak glows green
for a moment

Jeremy Rick
Portland, Oregon

leaf rain
settling the dusk
fireflies' light

r sorrels
Rocky Fork, Indiana

deep in the forest
a ladder of sunlight
I rise to the occasion

Theresa Mormino
Hot Springs, Arkansas

Spring
a new sun bonnet
changing the light

Merrill Gonzales
Dayville, Connecticut

gampi paper light through cherry blossoms

Terry Ann Carter
Victoria, British Columbia

Long dark shadow
on the Wall —
coyote

Jonathan Vos Post
Altadena, California

constant wind
the flag continues
to fray

Christopher Herold
Port Townsend, Washington

VRBO
turning the president's photo
to the wall

Caroline Giles Banks
Minneapolis, Minnesota

TV twitterstorm
I step outside to yell
at the starlings

Joan Prefontaine
Cottonwood, Arizona

an inmate's kite
impaled on razor wire
silent in summer twilight

Michael Kitchen
Chesterfield, Michigan

monarch waystation
a coil of rope
left behind

Bob Oliveira
Bonita Springs, Florida

snapping chalk lines as the crow flies

Rick Jackofsky
Rocky Point, New York

    clouds   white clouds
       rider on the horse
            now headless

Lidia Rozmus
Vernon Hills, Illinois

bow echo —
a sandhilll crane
blown off course

Robin White
Deerfield, New Hampshire

burning leaves
smokerise
in the slipstream of time

Harry Goodheart
Tryon, North Carolina

not flapping
against the strong sea breeze
the gull goes nowhere

Steven H. Greene
Haddon Township, New Jersey

early frost
the rustle between
blades of moonlight

Kathryn J. Stevens
Cary, North Carolina

at the top
of the totem pole —
raven on raven

Carole MacRury
Point Roberts, Washington

pumpkin patch
grown for competition
the scarecrow shows how big

Diane Wallihan
Port Townsend, Washington

spider legs
black on white tile
trick or treat

Marian M. Poe
Plano, Texas

attic mice nest in family secrets

Roberta Beach Jacobson
Indianola, Iowa

autumn evening
I visit her grave
two shadows

Randy Cadenhead
Decatur, Georgia

old memories
a squeaking screen door
bangs shut

Cheryl Berrong
Fairbanks, Alaska

spring birdsong
a merry-go-round needing oil
adds its notes

Steve Tabb
Boise, Idaho

outside the zendo
a dog barking, barking
inside the zendo, too

Don Wentworth
Pittsburgh, Pennsylvania

meditation . . .
the roar of a whisper
from the hallway

Elinor Pihl Huggett
Lakeville, Indiana

eyes closed
upping the volume
of the robin

Peter Newton
Winchendon, Massachusetts

nursing home visit
three tenors
snoring in unison

Patricia Harvey
East Longmeadow, Massachusetts

that song
heard in the morning . . .
and all day long

Elizabeth Fanto
Timonium, Maryland

one red tulip
blooms in the hosta border
time alone with God

Ellen Grace Olinger
Oostburg, Wisconsin

second hand moving the hum of a light bulb

Eric Jennings
Oakland, California

chasing the night —
a falling blossom
graces my tea

Mary Kendall
Chapel Hill, North Carolina

calm water
little hurries
where it's touched

Jeffrey Ferrara
Worcester, Massachusetts

you are now my friend
from another time and place
I tell the smooth rock

Aron Laub
Woodland Hills, California

how air and water
transfigures
morning mist

Harold Cowherd
East Lansing, Michigan

matcha bowl
the tempest preceding
tranquility

Tom Lyon Freeland
Edmonton, Alberta

a hot water bath
in the Valley of the Vapors
sacred to all tribes

Howard Lee Kilby
Hot Springs National Park, Arkansas

waterbuck saunter
through protesting reeds
crumpling the light

Lysa Collins
White Rock, British Columbia

Ancient water
skipping stones on
sunset reflections

R Michael Beatty
South Bend, Indiana

Flickering candles
the only light
in the dark, empty church

Juan Edgardo De Pascuale
Gambier, Ohio

she rests
among leaf patterns
recovery room

Paul Kulwatno
Falls Church, Virginia

stroke by stroke
the brush through
my mother's hair

Patty Hardin
Long Beach, Washington

prairie wind beating native drums

Dianne Koch
Dubuque, Iowa

the way a horse
can be perfectly still
and still wild

Bonnie Stepenoff
Chesterfield, Missouri

The rain
the same on all sides
of the house

Bruce England
Santa Clara, California

yellow maple
our edges
softer in the fog

Dianne Garcia
Seattle, Washington

a hole
deep in my pocket
last day of fall

Theresa A. Cancro
Wilmington, Delaware

one dry crack
on a hunting field
autumn settles

George Gerolimatos
Barrington, Illinois

november woods
the trail peppered
with turkey tracks

Mike Stinson
Omaha, Nebraska

path to my dogs' graves mulch deep with memory

Donna Bauerly
Dubuque, Iowa

the rush
through wet leaves
no crackle

Shelley Baker-Gard
Portland, Oregon

filling the orchard
with its presence
deer silence

Angela Terry
Lake Forest Park, Washington

autumn sunset
a cardinal spits out
the husk

Brad Bennett
Arlington, Massachusetts

turning seventy
candle wax
in the icing

Bob Whitmire
Round Pond, Maine

summer walk
my wife lends me
her walking stick

Edward J. Rielly
Westbrook, Maine

lost years
the search area
widens

LeRoy Gorman
Napanee, Ontario

travel mugs venn diagram the coffee table

kjmunro
Whitehorse, Yukon Territory

lengthening shadows
a raven
on the rooftop

Jone Rush MacCulloch
Happy Valley, Oregon

bald eagles mating
in mid-air, I spread my mind
wider and wider

Chen-ou Liu
Ajax, Ontario

spring dance
wallflowers sit alone
hoping to be picked

Christine Wenk-Harrison
Lago Vista, Texas

flying dragons rescued me
from you, my wayward prince
before you aged and faded

Clarise Samuels
Hudson, Québec

hellfire sermon
he hurriedly returns
my apple

Pris Campbell
Lake Worth, Florida

speaking
for themselves
wild orchids

Margo Williams
Stayton, Oregon

leaving him
while the lilacs
are not in bloom

Jill Lange
Cleveland Heights, Ohio

falling snow —
trying to find that place
in me

Sondra J. Byrnes
Santa Fe, New Mexico

snow-quieted world:
in a dream
I unfriend everyone

Susan Antolin
Walnut Creek, California

late sunlight
rakes the forest
chords on an old guitar

Robert Witmer
Tokyo, Japan

The arch of autumn leaves—
a cathedral in the yard
where I go to pray

Daniel A. Zehner
Woodstown, New Jersey

loon swims by
i hear her other voice
silence

Arch Haslett
Toronto, Ontario

the sun wobbling
in the water
lattices of light

Leanne Jaeger
Hobart, Tasmania, Australia

amplified by fog
in the leafless forest
wren song

Kristen Lindquist
Camden, Maine

haloed moon . . .
  from the cedar wafts
  the scent of thaw

Robert Gilliland
Austin, Texas

sugaring season
in the air
a quickening

Mary Frederick Ahearn
Pottstown, Pennsylvania

just enough spring
to bring mimosas
to the patio

Anna Eklund-Cheong
Croissy-sur-Seine, France

forsythia
in the circle drive
around and around and around

Barbara Robinette
Viola, Arkansas

plum blossoms
all the pumpkin flavors
on sale

jim rodriguez
Washougal, Washington

fingertips tell tales
of pansy petals
soft and wet with dew

Harold Feddersen
Terrace, British Columbia

your lush auburn hair —
the dog whines and scratches
at the door

Frank Judge
Rochester, New York

a towel
around the hips —
starry night

Luce Pelletier
Brossard, Québec

fragrance
of a thousand loves
redbud

Kath Abela Wilson
Pasadena, California

rose blush
the color of my cheeks
Sunday morning

Barbara Tate
Winchester, Tennessee

old perfume bottle
a hundred tiny rainbows
dance on the wall

Susan Spooner
Victoria, British Columbia

nape
of her neck
unwritten poem

Don Krutek
Egg Harbor, Wisconsin

a word
on the tip of my tongue
angle of repose

Barbara Snow
Eugene, Oregon

year in review
my word cloud full
of poetry

Margaret Dornaus
Ozark, Arkansas

night wind
my misplaced
apostrophes

Francine Banwarth
Dubuque, Iowa

G OD EATS an unlit O

Raymond C Roy
Winston-Salem, North Carolina

dusk settles
beyond the neon —
just one beer

K. O. Smith
Asheville, North Carolina

in a dark lounge
acquisition and merger
napkin-outlined

Barth H. Ragatz
Fort Wayne, Indiana

exploring the city
after dark
the moon

Sam Bateman
Everett, Washington

the wail of a sax
slows her crisp step
late night blues

Wanda Cook
Hadley, Massachusetts

darkness
incomplete without
the streetlight

Patti Niehoff
Cincinnati, Ohio

Lincoln Tunnel
a yellow Lamborghini
wakes up my inner child

Arlene Teck
Rockaway, New Jersey

behind the strip curtain
a baggage handler
opens and closes his hands

Steve Dolphy
Eastleigh, Hampshire, England

deep end of the night the first train home as empty

Adrian Bouter
Gouda, the Netherlands

dead of winter

wishing it was warm enough
to snow

Amelia Cotter
Chicago, Illinois

cold afternoon
the sigh of her down coat
as we embrace

Stephen Colgan
Oakland, California

bitter wind
on bare branches
plastic Easter eggs

Christina Laurie
Falmouth, Cape Cod, Massachusetts

winter sun
a shallow understanding
of the problem

Frank J. Tassone
Montebello, New York

passing ambulance
my dog's howling visible
in the freezing air

Art Elser
Denver, Colorado

ponytail clouds
in the winterblue sky
her peppermint kiss

Garry Wilson
Issaquah, Washington

a north wind
rearranging the leaves —
WestPac deployment

Cyndi Lloyd
Riverton, Utah

empty bedroom
sunlight slowly moves across
the dusty floor

Jeannette Hudyma
Olympia, Washington

mid-autumn
the hummingbird feeder
swings north, then south

Lynn Edge
Tivoli, Texas

the wooden door
certainly, the shadows
the iron lock   silence

Lemuel Waite
Georgetown, Kentucky

slice by slice
through window blinds
thunder clouds

Seretta Martin
San Diego, California

empty glasses —
she only left behind
her lipstick

Roy Kindelberger
Edmonds, Washington

at the table
his silence . . .
i stir my stew

Charlotte Digregorio
Winnetka, Illinois

the moon
narrower and narrower
this door toward divorce

Louisa Howerow
London, Ontario

cedar waxwings
in the crab apple tree
long-range plans

Gary Hittmeyer
Shokan, New York

storm clouds —
unable to navigate
her silence

Risë Daniels
Higganum, Connecticut

all I was able to give you   a rose's thorns

Ludmila Balabanova
Sofia, Bulgaria

rain shadow
neither of us cries
when we part

Katherine Raine
Milton, Otago, New Zealand

a moment's longing
     wind stirs
the potted geraniums

Ce Rosenow
Eugene, Oregon

unicycle sometimes I believe

Michelle Schaefer
Bothell, Washington

wild violets
beside Totoro's forest . . .
distant voices

Leanne Mumford
Sydney, New South Wales, Australia

birdsong
my chest expands
with one note

Debbi Antebi
London, England

the last bit
of lorem ipsum —
spring starlight

Cherie Hunter Day
Menlo Park, California

desert monolith tuning wind a pitch lower

Jo Balistreri
Waukesha, Wisconsin

prairie night
through the diesel's open chord
Orion

Ruth Yarrow
Ithaca, New York

indiangrass
parts and sways
the progress of a hare

Alanna C. Burke
Santa Fe, New Mexico

sunflowers
standing mute
in moonlight

Tom Habney
Bellingham, Washington

meteor shower
the click-clack
of a passing train

Joseph Fulkerson
Owensboro, Kentucky

whose door once opened
here, between two lilacs
in this empty field

Maggie Roycraft
Morristown, New Jersey

Valentine's Day —
tracing the razor scars
on my arm

Joshua Gage
Cleveland, Ohio

carrying
the weight of raindrops
evensong

Sneha Sundaram
Jersey City, New Jersey

geese
in free flight hardly
a shape to them

Peter Meister
New Hope, Alabama

canopy of warblers our silence

Deborah P Kolodji
Temple City, California

Lying all alone
Trying to connect the dots
Under the night sky

Veeraja R
Franklin, Tennessee

scattered light
turns dark into day
let the journey continue

Dale Kimball
Bellingham, Washington

first spring day
whatever it is
that wags a dog's tail

Billie Wilson
Juneau, Alaska

partridge
swaying on a bare branch—
I'm leaning into joy

Munira Judith Avinger
Lac Brome, Québec

spring stream
my body becomes
a chalice

Michael Sheffield
Santa Rosa, California

a quarter to dusk
fledgling bluebirds
join the riot in the birdbath

Elizabeth Howard
Arlington, Tennessee

whitewater
my body shaking
with laughter

Rob Grotke
Nevada City, California

heather slopes
carry me
valley to valley

Joanna Ashwell
Barnard Castle, England

Canadian hotel —
the little girl opens the curtains
to fireflies

Karen O'Leary
West Fargo, North Dakota

Taj Mahal —
a woman in a burqa
takes a selfie

Mykel Board
New York, New York

the internet stalls —
shades of autumn
colour the window

Madhuri Pillai
Melbourne, Victoria, Australia

crimson sunset
my shadow
missing yours

Tom Vorderer
Cambridge, Massachusetts

ambulance siren
the red tulips
open wider

Margaret Chula
Portland, Oregon

cherry blossoms
i dress myself
in pain patches

Michael Morell
Havertown, Pennsylvania

almost 80 . . .
new lenses to better see
the afterlife

George Swede
Toronto, Ontario

the kind voice
of the blood-pressure machine
winter night

David Oates
Athens, Georgia

Days of future past
Knights in white gowns
treading the urologist's hall

Mac Parks
Lakewood, Colorado

for a moment
it was an acid rock solo —
MRI

Marita Gargiulo
Hamden, Connecticut

hearing test —
the various white noises
of the HMO

Rick Clark
Seattle, Washington

banging into everything —
the elbow
in the sling

Pegi Deitz Shea
Vernon, Connecticut

gingko leaves
a wind chime knocks
on the empty house

Carmen Sterba
University Place, Washington

spring dawn
i stare at a blank page
while my tea steeps

Bona M. Santos
Los Angeles, California

raising the pitch too
high snaps the string   a cold rain
strips the final leaves

David Cashman
Providence, Rhode Island

the boots he wore
covered with dust
MIA

Charmaine Endres
Las Vegas, Nevada

National Cemetery
P-51 flyover
trailing smoke

Richard Tice
Kent, Washington

deafening geese fly
in victory formation
singing of the south

Andy Felong
Redwood City, California

winter stars
adjusting
my expectations

Michele L. Harvey
Hamilton, New York

Cherry tree's
Bare branches
Cold cup of tea

Michael Smith
Knoxville, Tennessee

distant phone call . . .
in our pauses
each other's crickets

Patricia McKernon Runkle
Short Hills, New Jersey

skin lost   words dropped from a tongue

Jean Aldriedge
Bellows Falls, Vermont

winding yarn
the knitting circle voices
go on and on

J Hahn Doleman
San Francisco, California

gardener speaks
to a struggling plant
in Mayan

Gil Jackofsky
San Marcos, California

bonsai exhibit
  the old man the same shape
    as his tree

Jerome Cushman
Victor, New York

even without apples
twisted branches find
the earth

Dina E Cox
Unionville, Ontario

lichened dead oak
elephanting across lake
kissing itself

Susan Lee Roberts
Sacramento, California

black mountain rocks
a little moss plant
spreads its leaves

Manoj Nair
Bangalore / India

a flower
stitched into a wash cloth
opens

Michael Fessler
Sagamihara, Japan

origami box
unfolding it and refolding it
with a defibrillator inside

Bruce H. Feingold
Berkeley, California

an eagle calls
my eyes
to the sky

Jacquie Pearce
Vancouver, British Columbia

ocean breeze
a seagull's wing tip
grazes the day moon

Terri L. French
Huntsville, Alabama

coastal winds toss
orange clouds into sunset
pelicans hold their course

Brady Rubin
Ashland, Oregon

Earth sonata
spiraling time-space
in the key of blue-green

Miriam Borne
New York, New York

after yoga~
tolling buoy
lulls me to sleep

Janis Albright Lukstein
Rancho Palos Verdes, California

Waves bring messages,
Mankind waits along the beach,
Those of peace still drown.

Arthur C. Ford, Sr.
Pittsburgh, Pennsylvania

dandelion grows
in the sidewalk crack —
smokestacks in bloom

William Seiyo Shehan
Chicago, Illinois

summer sun —
granite office buildings
fanned by ginkgo leaves

Joanne Szafran
Washington, District of Columbia

skyscraper
a crow hops down
from the curb

Chuck Brickley
Daly City, California

the mica
in the asphalt
Fifth Avenue

Judith Hishikawa
Astoria, New York

on Wall Street
a sparrow makes
a nest

Rita Gray
New York, New York

behind our
new municipal building —
tents of the homeless

Ruth Holzer
Herndon, Virginia

spring evening
the faces outside
the union hall

Nicholas M. Sola
New Orleans, Louisiana

may day
the neighbor's dog
slips his leash

Skaidrite Stelzer
Toledo, Ohio

kickboxing
in the night
cherry trees blossom.

Kendra E. Shaw
San Diego, California

two ropes turning
to the double Dutch beat
I spring into summer

Patricia Wakimoto
Gardena, California

waist deep in the Pacific
which way to swim
a whitecap decides

Mark Hurtubise
Spokane, Washington

summer breeze
rocking on the verandah
all the family ghosts

Antoinette Libro
St. Augustine, Florida

Post office . . .
long lines
short chats

David H. Rosen
Eugene, Oregon

over and over
the clock strikes
unafraid of watchers

John S. Gilbertson
Greenville, South Carolina

in the men's room
at Grand Central Station . . .
one hand on my luggage

John S Green
Bellingham, Washington

darker still
in the rearview mirror
a glimpse of me

Mark Osterhaus
Punta Gorda, Florida

twenty-fifth
high school reunion
. . . embers

William Scott Galasso
Laguna Woods, California

old photograph
in it i'm wearing the shirt
i'm wearing

Dana Grover
San Jose, California

mom's in the hospital
dad worries
he can't find his hat

> Jay Howard
> Springfield, Missouri

clear ice —
skating into
dad's perfect circle

> Laurie D. Morrissey
> Hopkinton, New Hampshire

the way Mom floated
a single camellia —
this clear glass bowl

> Mimi Ahern
> San Jose, California

winter's edge
our unused
bassinet

Gary Evans
Stanwood, Washington

foggy day—
back down from the attic
with more memories

Tom Clausen
Ithaca, New York

ebb tide
I scatter the ashes
of my childhood

Lorin Ford
Melbourne, Victoria, Australia

petals flutter down
the longest
six feet

Jim Kacian
Winchester, Virginia

soft summer rain
drips off the end of the leaf
his final IV

Karen DiNobile
Poughkeepsie, New York

my brother's passing—
force-blooming apple blossoms
by his picture

George Skane
Georgetown, Massachusetts

shimmering fog
sunshine burns through
the grief

Mary Weidensaul
Granby, Massachusetts

rising gongsound
into it I release
my burden

Connie Hutchison
Kirkland, Washington

Branch bends under weight
Springs back toward the deep blue sky
Steller's Jay takes flight

Alexis George
Bayside, California

spring equinox teetering on joy

Matthew Caretti
Mercersburg, Pennsylvania

a crossing guard
stops traffic
for cherry blossoms

Victor Ortiz
Bellingham, Washington

red tulips
setting off
all the alarms

Beverly Acuff Momoi
Mountain View, California

rash wind
lily pads
flash their backsides

Jennifer Thiermann
Glenview, Illinois

end of summer
the toddler reaching
for a doorknob

Bill Kenney
Whitestone, New York

that evening
our first grandson pointed
to the moon

Brenda Lempp
Madison, Wisconsin

schoolgirls jumping
              double Dutch
on the first day of spring

Anthony Franco
Jersey City, New Jersey

from seagull
    to seagull
        sunrise

Jeannie Martin
Arlington, Massachusetts

red yellow green
the shape
of a maple leaf

Chandra Bales
Albuquerque, New Mexico

how chicken feed
came in calico bags
my first quilt

Denise Fontaine-Pincince
Belchertown, Massachusetts

winter sleepover
defending my blanket fort
with throw pillows

Sari Grandstaff
Saugerties, New York

spring storms
power company's number
on speed dial

Dennise Aiello
Benton, Louisiana

in hurricane winds
the flags snap to attention —
miss harrison's ruler

Sharon Rhutasel-Jones
Los Ranchos, New Mexico

the morning after . . .
reshuffled trees reveal
a new piece of sky

Craig Kittner
Wilmington, North Carolina

drought—
in the sky a lightning bolt
shaped like a river

Corine Timmer
Estoi, Faro, Portugal

rolling hills
splayed with mustard blossoms
fire storm

Stevie Strang
Laguna Niguel, California

wildfire smoke
sets the moon ablaze
nighthawk ballet

Gary Bullock
Sequim, Washington

August heat
their fielder gets away with
trapping one

Dan Schwerin
Greendale, Wisconsin

the time it takes
to drive by the field
stand-up triple

Mark Dailey
Poultney, Vermont

small town ball field
a long home run
off a headstone

Frank Higgins
Kansas City, Missouri

cornfield
lit by fireflies
Christmas in June

Bette Hall-Munger
Clancy, Montana

perseid shower —
  among the shooting stars
a leisurely satellite

Frank K. Robinson
Knoxville, Tennessee

winter twilight clouds crashing our star party

James A. Paulson
Narberth, Pennsylvania

day break moon
snapping a key
in the lock

Michael Henry Lee
Saint Augustine, Florida

ghost town
loose window shutters creak
in a hot desert wind

Gerald A. McBreen
Pacific, Washington

cherry petals
on the monument of mass hysteria
four-decades old

Tadao Okazaki
Fukushima, Japan

quantum jitters
these random social
interactions

Lesley Anne Swanson
Coopersburg, Pennsylvania

during pauses
in our phone call
prayer-bead clicks

Thomas Chockley
Plainfield, Illinois

coldest night
bark of a guard dog
once

Roland Packer
Hamilton, Ontario

winters so cold that
breath freezes solid —
wet matches

Jim Bloss
Monroe, Washington

scuba diving test
despite the frosty air — son
drops into the lake

Jeanne Jorgensen
Edmonton, Alberta

flakes small as sand
falling for days
snowed in

C. J. Prince
Bellingham, Washington

ungroomed trail
the tyke's cross-country skis
constantly cross

Margaret Rutley
Bridgewater, Nova Scotia

Light snowfall
I sweep
for the crows

Linda Thompson
Colorado Springs, Colorado

Easter morning
a fresh path
through the snow

Julie Warther
Dover, Ohio

spring equinox
my dying friend's
open door

Matt Cariello
Bexley, Ohio

the wind flows
through the meadow
wild violets

Sharon Lynne Yee
Torrance, California

hospice window
dawn gives shape
to the trees

Lynne Steel
Coral Springs, Florida

my father dies
while I lecture about
impermanence

David G. Lanoue
New Orleans, Louisiana

harvest moon
the ferris wheel rolls away
passengerless

Jeffrey McMullen
Cuba, New York

camouflaging
my grief
a seed catalog

Jon Hare
Falmouth, Massachusetts

weeding
if only to hear
the song sparrow

Anne E. Burgevin
Pennsylvania Furnace, Pennsylvania

after the war . . .
deciding the dandelions
are flowers

Steve Hodge
White Lake, Michigan

garden Buddha
placid
in green silences

Fred Andrle
Columbus, Ohio

hazy cherry blossoms —
waiting for perfect words to spring up

Atsuko Mine
Matsumoto, Nagano, Japan

goldfish pond my wishes disappear one by one

Susan Beth Furst
Woodbridge, Virginia

tulips nipped in bud
just deserts for local deer
through an open gate

Alice Mallory
Ashland, Oregon

heron
in the creek   watches . . .
spring-hued willows

Patricia Nolan
Colorado Springs, Colorado

log of turtles
scene to unseen
less than a second

Ann M. Penton
Green Valley, Arizona

a black swallowtail drifts
clouds cross sun and treetops
lilacs cast shadows

Kia Hayes
Philadelphia, Pennsylvania

Bluebird dives
lands on birdhouse
worm squirms

John-Carl Davis
West Bend, Wisconsin

in the pasture
milk cows grazing
wild garlic growing

Wilma McCracken
Downers Grove, Illinois

spring dawn
birdsong before
the alarm goes off

John Quinnett
Bryson City, North Carolina

an owl
only my children can hear
morning rush

Tia Haynes
Lakewood, Ohio

six windows
two tellers
the line grows longer

Mike Schoenburg
Skokie, Illinois

digging for change
I pick around
the new penny

Ida Freilinger
Redmond, Washington

waiting for
the fog to lift —
migraine

Barbara Hay
Tulsa, Oklahoma

arctic eve
a sun too tired
to set

C.R. Harper
Mill Creek, Washington

long day
taking clothes off the line
by moonlight

Linda Ahrens
Arlington, Texas

off-season
the sunset
so-so

Roberta Beary
Westport, County Mayo, Ireland

lonely nights —
still sleeping on just my side
of the bed

Vernon Chain
Waynesboro, Mississippi

deep winter
enough snow
to hide the neighbors

Ignatius Fay
Sudbury, Ontario

winter cricket
halfway up a kitchen wall
we see eye to eye

James Won
Temple City, California

the to-do list
gets shorter
winter solstice

Joan Chaput
Glastonbury, Connecticut

black pine, old pine
in the night woods
a new year begins

Ellen Ankenbrock
Washougal, Washington

first dream
I sit with my grandfathers
speaking Michif

Phillip Kennedy
Monterey, California

first day of the year
cigarette smoke and pine drift
into our promises

Shasta Hatter
Portland, Oregon

a cloud of pollen
from the cedar . . .
memories of Mom

Connie Donleycott
Bremerton, Washington

redwood forest
each tree its own story . . .
rare book collection

Kendall Lott
Bloomington, Indiana

broken chainsaw
rusting in the rain
stumps sprout new shoots

Charles Harmon
Whittier, California

the slender twig
bends with the hummingbird's weight —
lifting fog

Sharon Hammer Baker
Findlay, Ohio

monk seal flipper
so like my hand
an itch under a chin

Carole Slesnick
Bellingham, Washington

dry stone wall
one by one the hens
go broody

Vanessa Proctor
Sydney, New South Wales, Australia

walking past
a barbed wire fence
quails sound the alarm

Kathryn Bold
Coto de Caza, California

heavy traffic
doe on the shoulder
waiting to cross

donna pohlmann
Sioux Falls, South Dakota

death of a young rabbit
the quarter moon
its primary witness

Betty Hartnett
Wayzata, Minnesota

Earth Day
a poet's instructions
on how to skin a snake

Carolyn Hall
San Francisco, California

deep
purple
columbine
breach
births
a
bee

Tanya McDonald
Woodinville, Washington

stepping into the stillness   opossum

Ben Moeller-Gaa
St. Louis, Missouri

ferry unloading
yellow-bellied newts
crossing the road

Ann Spiers
Vashon Island, Washington

news of the bees . . .
forgiving them
their stings

Bill Pauly
Asbury, Iowa

cruise ship gala
a mylar ribbon snares
the mollymawk's wing

Vicki Miko
Costa Mesa, California

we bury the hawk
with her missing talons
grey dawn

Marilyn Ashbaugh
Edwardsburg, Michigan

London suburb —
a long conversation
between magpies

Sharon R. Wesoky
Meadville, Pennsylvania

blazing row
the dog gets
another walk

David J Kelly
Dublin, Ireland

after our quarrel
you pull a snagged thread back
into your sweater

Olivier Schopfer
Geneva, Switzerland

sorting darks and lights
my love note
in his pocket

Robyn Hood Black
Beaufort, South Carolina

my grumpy neighbor
smiles
cactus blossom

Barbara Sabol
Akron, Ohio

in-law's visit
the mockingbird
at it again

Bryan Rickert
Belleville, Illinois

Complementary
Gossip and ghosts
Spring haircut

Jill Whalen
Waukesha, Wisconsin

hedge trimming
in the garden
a deer

Joan Marie Roberts
Victoria, British Columbia

spring evening
a tadpole swims
across the moon

Randall Herman
Victoria, Texas

a fissure
in February
crocus in bloom

Nancy Shires
Greenville, North Carolina

a red chorus of roses
lifted by the wind

Cheryl Pfeil von der Heyde
Greenbrae, California

a light dusting
coats cars canary yellow
a chameleon hides

Patricia Cruzan
Fayetteville, Georgia

a dirt smudge
on the toddler's nose
crocus shoots

Matthew Moffett
Mt. Pleasant, Michigan

my glasses . . .
viewing my world
through the baby's prints

Dorothy McLaughlin
Somerset, New Jersey

boosting his child
over the puddle
airplane wings!

Ronald K. Craig
Batavia, Ohio

third eye —
my grandson discovers a flashlight

Cynthia Gallaher
Chicago, Illinois

first braces . . .
a puffin's beak fringed
with silver

Debbie Strange
Winnipeg, Manitoba

babysitting —
learning the name
of each unicorn

Julie Bloss Kelsey
Germantown, Maryland

tropical vacation
birds of paradise
in the hotel lobby

Mark Hitri
Fort Worth, Texas

salvation
I slap myself for killing
a mosquito

Srinivasa Rao Sambangi
Hyderabad, Telangana, India

storefront reflection
consumes
a good part of me

Michael J. Galko
Houston, Texas

green press conference
coffee
in foam cups

jimhaynes/jimu
Knoxville, Tennessee

lunch at last
dad slots his hearing aid
in record time

David Jacobs
London, England

hoarfrost
after buttering the bread
I notice the mold

Oleg Kagan
Los Angeles, California

Vegas
her winning
smile

Robert Epstein
El Cerrito, California

gleaming tulip beds
a woman checks her teeth
for lipstick smears

Amy Losak
Teaneck, New Jersey

green frog on red leaf
riveting

robyn corum
Hartselle, Alabama

meditation . . .
loosening a *not*
in my stomach

Sidney Bending
Victoria, British Columbia

forest bathing . . .
no one mentioned
black flies

Nika
Calgary, Alberta

late snowfall
below the ridgeline
her lost panties

John Budan
Newberg, Oregon

cherry blossoms
then no cherry blossoms
deleted email

Neal Whitman
Pacific Grove, California

longest night
the far-off lights
of passing ships

Dan Curtis
Victoria, British Columbia

hazy moon
counting the days
backwards

Mark Forrester
Hyattsville, Maryland

retirement spring
red-winged blackbirds
sing in the wetland

Susan Farner
Urbana, Illinois

a night rain
that moistens plums but doesn't
raise the river

Burnell Lippy
Danville, Vermont

autumn evening
a leaf rests on a rock
above the falls

Michael Ketchek
Rochester, New York

long-legged spider
outside the kitchen window
hard frost predicted

David Berger
Seattle, Washington

ice fishing
a blue heron steps
across the pond

Jim Laurila
Florence, Massachusetts

December deepfreeze . . .
pinecones on the snow crust
gnawed into drumsticks

Michael Dudley
Peterborough, Ontario

snow day —
I spend it worrying
about the hummingbirds

C. R. Manley
Bellevue, Washington

eight degrees
sun ripples on the raven's
glonk glonk

Elizabeth Hazen
Williston, Vermont

in golden sticks of moonshine
wolf's legs
light the night

Frances Farrell
Coon Rapids, Minnesota

wing shadows
        flicker on the snow
not a bird in flight

Marshall Hryciuk
Toronto, Ontario

moonlight haloing
snowy mountain peaks
eerie winds

Ruth Marcus
Sequim, Washington

winter light
shines on a nest of dryer lint—
stillborn mice

R. J. Swanson
Rollingbay, Washington

clinging
to the surface of things . . .
melting snow

Stella Pierides
Neusaess, Germany and London, England

with snow onto a lake
soft polka dots
are hanging out

Ryoko Suzuki
Otsu, Shiga, Japan

sudden thaw
we look for the snowman
in the river

Barry Goodmann
Hackensack, New Jersey

softened inner tube's
slow turns . . .
summer winding down

jeff stillman
Hobe Sound, Florida

last day of summer
funneling down the chimney
Vaux's swifts

Alan S. Bridges
Littleton, Massachusetts

down and back
along the washed-out road
a brown bat

paul m.
Bristol, Rhode Island

wild mountain iris
the color of the first time
we climbed together

J. Zimmerman
Santa Cruz, California

the vague trail opens
on a blue and white glen
scent of lupine

Al Gallia
Lafayette, Louisiana

raindrop on a rose leaf all i want to take with me

Tzetzka Ilieva
Marietta, Georgia

there is no world
outside of this—
cherry blossom

thomasjohnwellsmiller
Aptos, California

finding peace
in this unremarkable moment
pampas grass

Kelly Sauvage Angel
Madison, Wisconsin

leaf blower shuts off
now it's just the window fan
and the chickadees

Chad Henry
Aurora, Colorado

Slapping my neck
At phantom mosquitoes not there

Tim Alley
Ehime, Japan

trying to sleep in my ear cat whiskers

Jackie Maugh Robinson
Las Vegas, Nevada

the touch
of caterpillar bristles
marshmallow blooms

Anna Cates
Wilmington, Ohio

following the scent
deep in the garden
I become a butterfly

Fay Aoyagi
San Francisco, California

mason jar
never enough
holes

Joe McKeon
Strongsville, Ohio

midlife
trying to outrun
a deer fly

Deb Koen
Rochester, New York

checking out
farewell to the hotel's
bathtub spider

Sheila Sondik
Bellingham, Washington

a branch cloaked
in webworms
autumn chill

Lori Becherer
Millstadt, Illinois

angelus bells —
staring out the window
at an empty street

Tim Happel
Iowa City, Iowa

the notes
from a saxophone
spiraling smoke

Claire Vogel Camargo
Austin, Texas

shadow waltz —
bare branches
and the moonbeam

Maureen Lanagan Haggerty
Madison, New Jersey

after icarus —
a cedar waxwing
flying at sunset

Keith Polette
El Paso, Texas

murmuration at day's end Mozart softly played

Ellen Compton
Washington, District of Columbia

Last Post
wind
in the open mic

Hans Jongman
Welland, Ontario

tilled fields
in fallen rain
rows of sunrise

Warren Decker
Izumi, Osaka, Japan

sea waves
corrugate
the moon

Ann Rawson
Scotland

plumes of pampas grass
backlit—
incandescent bulbs

Suzanne Niedzielska
Glastonbury, Connecticut

ocotillo
clouds leave their shadows
on the land

Karina M. Young
Salinas, California

desert bird
dusk comes in colours
with no name

Sandi Pray
St. Johns, Florida

morning dew spices and oils the first crocus

∂ w skrivseth
St. Anthony, Minnesota

thriving in my yard
wild violets
my neighbor banished

John J. Han
Manchester, Missouri

shoplifting
the blue of blue jays
storm clouds

Doris Lynch
Bloomington, Indiana

the flavor of these woods
in a steady rain
neutrinos

Robert Forsythe
Annandale, Virginia

I pour jasmine tea
from the cast iron teapot
summer jazz

Lenard D. Moore
Raleigh, North Carolina

shy smile light as a feather as a refugee

Lee Gurga
Piatt County, Illinois

Index of Poets